THE SECRET WEAPON OF WEALTH

I0490820

Revealing the secrets and hidden meanings of money

By

Mr. Thomas Boaz

Table of content

INRODUCTION. ··4

PHASE 1 : ··6

WEALTH CREATION . ··································6

PHASE 2 : ···10

    What kind of strategies or tactics, moves around

WEALTH CREATION. ·································10

PHASE 3 : ···14

What are the 3 main principles for wealth creation: Secret

in building WEALTH. ································14

PHASE 4 : ···20

What are the solutions to this fundamental problem ? ··20

    ⬚ Are there any fastest way to build wealth ?········20

    ⬚ Can wealth be created from Nothing ? ············22

    ⬚ What is the main goal of wealth creation?········40

PHASE 5 : ···42

The secret weapon of the rich ····················42

CONCLUSION ···50

INRODUCTION

WHAT IS WEALTH ?

The essential issue in **Adam Smith's** definition is **wealth creation**. Verifiably, Smith distinguished wealth from government assistance. He expected to be that " the more well off a country turns into the more joyful are its residents". In this way, it is essential to figure out how a country can be rich. *Economics* is the subject that lets us know how to make a country well-off.

Robert Kiyosaki characterized wealth as the quantity of days you can get by without truly working, or without anybody in your family really working, yet still keeping up with your way of life.

In any case, for **Karl Marx**, wealth is something beyond an assortment of wares possessed by capital and esteemed in cash. That is the structure that wealth takes under private enterprise. Wealth is the gathering of items and exercises that addresses human issues; for example the gathering of purpose values.

All in all, **wealth** is the overflow of important monetary resources or actual belongings that can be transformed into a structure that can be utilized for exchanges.

PHASE 1 :

WEALTH CREATION ?

W ealth creation is the process of generating

wealth through the production of goods and
services, the acquisition of assets, or the
accumulation of financial capital. It is an
important concept in economics and is often used
to measure the success of an economy. Wealth
creation can be achieved through a variety of
methods, including investment, entrepreneurship,
and innovation.

Investment is one of the *most common methods
of wealth creation.* Investment involves the
purchase of assets such as stocks, bonds, and real
estate, which can then be used to generate income

or capital gains. Investment can also be used to purchase businesses or start-up companies, which can then be used to generate profits.

Entrepreneurship is another way to create wealth. Entrepreneurs create businesses that produce goods and services, which can then be sold to generate profits. Entrepreneurship requires risk-taking and creativity, and can be a great way to create wealth.

Innovation is also a key factor in wealth creation. Innovation involves the development of new products, services, or processes that can be used to generate profits. Innovation can be achieved through research and development, or through the use of existing technologies.

Finally, wealth creation can also be achieved through the accumulation of financial capital.

Financial capital can be generated through savings, investments, and other forms of financial planning. Financial capital can then be used to purchase assets or start businesses, which can then be used to generate profits.

Overall, wealth creation is an important concept in economics and is essential for the growth and development of an economy. It can be achieved through a variety of methods, including investment, entrepreneurship, and innovation.

Mr. Thomas Boaz

PHASE 2 :

What kind of strategies or tactics, moves around WEALTH CREATION ?

One of the **most important strategies** for wealth creation is to *save* and *invest* regularly. This means setting aside a portion of your income each month and investing it in assets that have the potential to generate returns. This could include stocks, bonds, mutual funds, real estate, and other investments. **It is important to diversify your investments so that you are not overly exposed to any one asset class**.

Another strategy for wealth creation is to **start a business**. Starting a business can be a great way to generate wealth, as it allows you to leverage your skills and knowledge to create a product or service that can generate income. **It is important to do your research and develop a business plan before starting a business, as this will help you to understand the risks and rewards associated with the venture.**

A third strategy for wealth creation is to **reduce expenses**. This means cutting back on unnecessary spending and focusing on essential expenses. This can help to free up more money to be invested in assets that can generate returns. **It is also important to pay off any high-interest debt, as this can help to reduce the amount of money that is being spent on interest payments.**

Finally, it is important to have a **long-term plan** for wealth creation. This means *setting goals* and *developing a plan* to achieve them. This could include setting a target retirement age, investing in assets that can generate returns, and diversifying your Investments. **It is also important to review your plan regularly and make adjustments as needed.**

Overall, wealth creation is a long-term process that requires careful planning and execution. There are many strategies that can be used to create wealth, including saving and investing regularly, starting a business, reducing expenses, and having a long-term plan. It is important to do your research and develop a plan that is tailored to your individual needs and goals.

Mr. Thomas Boaz

PHASE 3 :

The 3 main principles for wealth creation: Secret in building WEALTH.

Although there isn't a single formula for accumulating wealth, there are certain principles that must be followed. These are the three key secret disciplines that you must learn if you want to increase your riches.

- Save and Invest your money
- Put off satisfaction
- Ignore the Joneses

1. Discipline to Save and Invest your money.

We are completely restricted by the quantity of years we must have the option to go around effectively. A twenty-year-old today presumably has another 20–30 years of dynamic working life left. This is to say, as we age, the actual work we can offer diminishes. This period is the point at which we can set the foundation of our abundance.

The second you have chosen to make your abundance, you ought to make a move towards getting it going by beginning a dedicated investment account. Independent of the sum you choose to save intermittently, your reserve funds ought to be computerized to make it simpler to achieve discipline and consistency. You ought to likewise put your cash in amazing open doors like common assets and different ventures.

Currently, when picking a bank account, it is essential to track down one with negligible charges and impressive returns. Your set-aside money shouldn't sit in a bank; it ought to work for you to produce returns. For example, assuming that you set aside 1 million Dollar in 2017 at a 10% premium per annum, after one year, the cash ought to have expanded without anyone else to 1.1 million Dollar. This is the means by which you develop wealth consistently. Evaluate Cowrywise today.

2. Discipline to put off satisfaction.

If you look around, you probably see a lot of advertisements aimed at getting us to spend money on things we don't really need. There is no end to the new iPhone, cars, designer labels, shoes, and other products.

If you want to be rich one day, you should learn to put off buying these things until you have enough

money saved. This does not mean that you shouldn't take pleasure in the little pleasures of life. The point is that you always have the option of delaying the purchase of luxuries until you achieve important financial objectives. You should learn to live very low-income lives.

Or, even better, inquire as follows: Is this a necessity for my survival? Does this item increase my cash flow? Do I want to wow my friends by purchasing this?

3. Discipline to ignore the Joneses.

We are surrounded by the Joneses. They are the friends and families who spend money solely for the purpose of impressing others. Our neighbours who have a lot of flashy toys, our friends who buy the newest gadgets to show off, and our friends who barely have enough money to pay their rent to be like the Joneses.

To be like the Joneses means spending the little money you have saved on what the Joneses are buying. We always make poor financial decisions that are detrimental to building wealth as a result of this never-ending race to be like the Joneses.

It is essential to ensure that we are not attempting to live our lives as dictated by others before making any purchasing decisions. We need to learn how to budget effectively.

Mr. Thomas Boaz

PHASE 4 :

What are the solutions to these fundamental problem ?

- **What is the fastest way to build wealth?**

People all over the region do ask these questions a lot, trying to find the fastest way to create wealth. Well, However there are still ways one can get in building up wealth in a quick and efficient form ;

➢ Spend less than you earn.
➢ Stay within your means.
➢ The remainder should be set aside and invested for long-term growth.

That is how you swiftly amass wealth. However, many people, because they continue to spend more than they make, never truly accumulate money. Later in life, they are then financially supported in retirement by a pension or their offspring.

● How do you create wealth from nothing?

Can wealth be created from nothing? Is it possible to become rich while having no resources or cash at hand? Does the power of wealth come from having no capital? These are questions that confuse a lot of individuals around the country. On this page, we'll look at 8 doable measures you can take right away to start building wealth from scratch and start moving in the direction of a more financially free existence.

1. Learn about money and the principles of wealth creation.

Our mentality is generally the principal thing that needs to change before we can genuinely move toward any bigger changes in our lives.

"Everybody can fabricate a monetary ark to get by and prosper from now on," said **Robert Kiyosaki**, industry icon and creator of **Rich Dad, Poor Dad**. "However, you should focus profoundly on your monetary instruction to fabricate an ark with a strong groundwork."

The initial step to creating financial momentum from nothing is to concentrate on your monetary training. Get comfortable with fundamental terms like "pay," "costs, total assets," "profit from venture," "automated revenue," and "monetary freedom," among others.

Understand books, pay attention to unit projects and meetings, take courses, and follow monetary training online journals like Sarwa's.

Remember that monetary instruction, similar to each sort of schooling, should be a non-stop action. Learn constantly.

Be that as it may, a fair warning is significant here. The democratization of monetary data implies there is a ton of mistaken data out there.

You can follow trustworthy online journals that will give verifiable data and direct you to assets from trusted and fruitful financial backers, money managers, and monetary counsellors.

2. Find a reliable source of income.

Creating financial stability from nothing without a standard type of revenue is hard. You can't put money away without setting aside cash, and you can't set aside cash without a normal pay-check.

This is to say that individuals don't create feasible financial stability through staggered advertising, Ponzi schemes, or wagering.

Figure out how to overlook individuals who advance pyramid schemes that create financial well-being by simply working three hours every week. Practical wealth comes from building esteem over the long haul. On the off chance that you are not making natural worth and procuring pay from that great or administration, creating practical financial well-being is genuinely incomprehensible.

So find a decent line of work on the off chance that you don't have one and keep your work in the event that you really do have one.

On the off chance that you are an entrepreneur, keep zeroing in on building all the more long-term equity. "All wealth comes from adding esteem," said **Brian Tracy**, a self-improvement master, which incorporates laying out a plan of action that can "produce more, be better, be less expensive, be quicker, and be simpler than another person."

3. Set up a budget.

Setting up a financial plan and adhering to it are urgent if you have any desire to know how to create financial stability from nothing.

Utilizing that standard pay source we just discussed, you want to make a financial plan to assume control over how you are spending your cash, which is normally set consistently.

A financial plan is a monetary arrangement for a characterized period that contains assessed pay and uses for that period.

Each family or potentially individual necessities to make basically a month to month financial plan to distinguish their normal pay and assessed consumptions. *Living without a legitimate spending plan is like cruising without a compass*, and you can ensure that you'll lose all sense of direction in the ocean of monetary slip-ups.

A well-known planning procedure is the **50:30:20 rule**. In this method, you can figure out a financial plan where half of pay goes to fundamental costs (lease, contract, food, medical care), 30% to trivial items like shopping, excursion, diversion, and 20% to reserve funds and speculations.

Why is budgeting important?

One major factor is that it's easier to find areas where you can minimize costs when you understand how you spend your money. The more you increase your savings and investments, the smaller your spending must be.

You can increase your money more quickly by recognizing and eliminating needless and avoidable charges. It's that easy.

[For more on budgeting, read "How to Budget and Save Money"].

4. Obtain sufficient insurance (but don't go overboard)

One essential thing you ought to have in your spending plan is protection. Protecting yourself and your fundamental resources (properties, vehicles, and so forth) keeps you from bringing about gigantic misfortunes on account of unwanted occasions.

At least, you ought to have medical coverage so you don't burn through every last cent in the lamentable case of an expensive sickness. On the off chance that you don't have one, have an examination and look at medical coverage plans in the UAE and pick the one that is best for you.

In the event that you own your home and a vehicle, think about property owner's and collision protection. Additionally, assuming you have children and other family members, consider investing in term life insurance.

Creating financial well-being is great, yet it will be horrifying if you lose it to unexpected conditions and occasions. So be proactive and guarantee the things that are generally important to you.

In any case, don't over-safeguard. There are numerous protection items out there that are pointless. Adhere to the four above, except if there is a totally valid justification to get more.

"Purchasing protection can't transform you, yet it keeps it from being changed," said **Jack Ma**, the pioneer behind Alibaba and the most extravagant man in China. "You won't fail in light of the fact that you purchased protection; however, you will make your friends and family fail in the event that you don't."

5. Make "severe" financial sacrifices from your income.

While the **50:30:20** rule is a decent spot to begin, you'll find that you can save significantly more assuming that you set forth the energy.

Whenever you are focused on creating financial momentum, there will be numerous things in your spending plan that you can lessen or cut. You won't be the only one to do so. Today, there is no lack of networks that elevate ways of rehearsing "outrageous" reserve funds.

The "monetary autonomy, resign early" development, known as **FIRE**, is among the most famous.

They advance "outrageous" investment fund techniques that urge disciples to save a colossal amount of their month-to-month pay.

Jacob Doofus Fisker, one of the FIRE development's originators, proposed (and rehearsed) a technique that called for financial planning of 60% to 80% of one's month-to-month pay. Fisker wound up resigning at 33 years old and presently lives on $7,000 per year beyond Chicago.

Fisker (and different forerunners in the FIRE development) have developed enormous networks in view of the progress of their individual accounting examinations to eliminate costs (and the commercialization that ratchets them up).

They do this in different ways, including by building and making things they need rather than continuously getting them (e.g., baking bread, building tables). Aside from the monetary advantages, **Fisker** likewise gets a feeling of achievement, which he sees as more remunerating than industrialism.

[More deeply study these super saving tips by perusing Sarwa's meeting with Jacob Numskull Fisker]

While saving 60% to 80% of your pay may be too grand an objective for the present, essentially it lets you know that there are numerous valuable open doors for eliminating costs that you have most likely not yet investigated.

6. Create an emergency fund.

*Since you have figured out how to save a critical piece of your pay, the following strategy to create financial stability from nothing is to make a **secret stash**.*

A **secret stash** is like self-supported protection. It's cash you put away for surprising costs like vehicle fixes and unexpected conditions like employment cutbacks or pandemic-actuated lock-downs.

At the point when startling costs and unanticipated conditions emerge, there are ways of exacerbating the situation: cause obligation or potentially sell your investment(s).

You pay revenue on obligation, and when you sell your investment(s), you lose both the sum you sold and the premium from the market openness it might have acquired on the off chance that you didn't sell.

Hence, to stay away from those two situations, we prescribe that you figure out how to begin a secret stash immediately. A backup stash ought to be kept somewhere in the range of three and a half years' worth of your month-to-month expenses. Likewise, guarantee those assets are in an investment account where you can easily access them when the need arises.

Like protection, a just-in-case account won't make you rich; however, it will keep you from selling your speculations or bringing about obligations during crises.

7. Develop your skill set.

Reduce your spending or improve your income to increase your savings and investments. Although the latter needs equal attention to the former, many financial counsellors concentrate on the former.

If you are employed, broaden your skill set by enrolling in professional training programs and actively pursuing ongoing professional development. You can gain promotions or better job offers from other organizations by developing your talents (both hard and soft), which translates into more income.

If you run a small firm, increase your market knowledge, allocate more funds to innovation, and give your clients more value. You can do this to grow your market share and generate more income.

8. Consider ideas for passive income.

You should look into a variety of passive income opportunities in addition to increasing your employment or business income.

In contrast to your job or business, **passive income** is income that does not require your continuous presence or labour.

For those of us who are learning how to build wealth from nothing, passive income is essential. **Warren Buffett**, the legendary investor and CEO of Berkshire Hathaway, famously stated, "You will work until you die if you don't find a way to make money while you sleep."

Passive income can be divided into two categories: **investment passive income**, in which your money takes care of everything, and **non-investment passive income**, in which you do some side work. We'll stick with the latter here because the former is the focus of the following section.

In today's global and digital economy, there are numerous side hustle opportunities. Be wary, however, of schemes that promise to make quick money, such as betting websites and Ponzi schemes, when looking into these opportunities.

Some reliable and proven passive income ideas include:

• Selling digital products: Create digital items on topics that attract people if you are an authority in a particular niche, such as books, video courses, email courses, or paid webinars. The benefit of digital goods is that they only require a single creation (except for later updates). You can make money from a single product for a very long time.

• Blogging:You can market your concept through a series of regular blog entries rather than as a digital product. Once your blog has a significant amount of traffic, you may monetize it using a variety of methods, including Google Adsense, digital goods, paid membership, sponsorships, and guest posts.

- Affiliate marketing: You can resell other merchants' products and get paid a commission for each sale instead of selling your own digital goods on your blog. By using affiliate marketing, you can avoid having to develop your own product.
- Dropshipping: Dropshipping allows you to sell other merchants' products without having to purchase them yourself. You get an order from a consumer, process it with the producer, and then have the customer receive their order from the producer. Your income is the difference between the purchase price (which you pay to the merchant) and the retail price (which the client pays).

Mr. Thomas Boaz

- ## What is the main goal of wealth creation?

Individuals frequently can't help thinking about why the rich continue to get more extravagant.

Do the rich have some mystery ingredient that permits them to keep on driving their wealth year over year while the typical individual battles to take care of their bills and save for retirement?

Eventually, on the off chance that you're expecting an enchanted wealth mixture or mystery, indeed, Please accept my apologies since you will get disappointed.There's no mystery ingredient. Despite the fact that this the vast majority need, hustle and methodology are the keys to progress.

Making wealth is about steadily putting resources into yourself, instruction, and information, learning the essentials of funds, grasping gamble and award,

furthermore, facing proper challenges where required.Once you have those mechanics, it's tied in with utilizing your abundance by effective money management fittingly and acquiring out-sized returns. That, basically, is the technique for abundance creation.

Assuming you do the above again and again, you will create generational financial stability that will expand well past your lifetime, and reach out to your main beneficiaries.

At the point when I expound on making riches, I centre around the top 0.1%. I'm not alluding to a couple of million bucks, yet rather, $30 million and that's just the beginning (the top 0.1%). That is the wealth you need to accomplish, and that is the very thing that I compose about. **How to turn into a decamillionaire**

Mr. Thomas Boaz

PHASE 5 :

The secret weapon of the rich

Have you at any point wanted that there were 25 hours in a day? Can we just be real, there are days that regardless of what you do, you basically can't finish all that you needed to.

In the event that this sounds like you, you are in good company. Numerous entrepreneurs feel overpowered at some point in their business. It resembles a back-and-forth game where you are being pulled in such countless bearings that you never appear to finish anything.

Couldn't it be ideal to have a clear-cut advantage to assist you with winning this battle for your time? Here is the uplifting news: There is a clear-cut advantage you can utilize, and it's not difficult to set in motion.

The "clear-cut advantage" is called influence. By utilizing the force of influence, you can soar the development of your business. Influence is involving others or assets such that produces undeniably a larger number of results than how much exertion you need to exhaust.

Influence is the clear-cut advantage that the most well off individuals use to develop any sort of business they at any point have. Furthermore, influence can be your distinct advantage as well.

Let's look at **three strategies** you can use to tap into the power of leverage for yourself.

Leverage The Power of "People" as Your First Strategy.

It is hard to be aware or do everything yourself, particularly with the different undertakings that should be finished to work your business. That is where utilizing others becomes basic.

The primary method for utilizing individuals is to use outside project workers. You ought to designate all that you can to other people so you can zero in on the most basic piece of the business that no one but you can do. You ought to begin with project workers first, since you can employ them on a venture-by-venture basis.

The advantage of utilizing project workers is that you can enlist them without a drawn-out responsibility, similar to what a representative would require. This gives you the adaptability to take an alternate route without the pressure of letting workers go and all of the problems that go with it. Particularly while your business is new, hiring workers is an incredible method for finishing the work.

You might think, "I sure have no issue designating others, yet I can't bear to do as such." If this is true, you are in good company, since that is a typical response. The extraordinary news is that it doesn't need to be costly to employ individuals or organizations to help you.

For instance, a few undertakings you might require done will require one expertise, while different tasks might require another ability. Extraordinary hotspots for finding project workers incorporate Fiverr.com and Freelancer.com. **Fiverr** is an incredible site that permits you to get different kinds of tasks finished for just $5 per project.

At the point when you are prepared for representatives, you can find the perfect individual through references from others you know, through work sites like Monster.com, or from online and print advertising.

Leverage The Power Of "Your Time" as Part Of Strategy 2.

One more method for involving the force of influence in your business is to use your time. You can utilize time for your potential benefit, but you can likewise utilize it to your detriment.

For instance, assuming you are continually permitting yourself to be intruded on in your line of reasoning, at that point, you may just get a small portion of the outcomes that you could get on the off chance that you were completely engaged.

What these interruptions can prompt is either the inclination that you lack the capacity to deal with anything (even loved ones), or they can prompt the final product that things take way longer than they ought to finish.

In the event that this happens to you, contemplate utilizing the **80/20 Rule**. As indicated by the **80/20 Rule**, at times referred to **Pareto's Law** as, "20% of the things you really do prompt 80% of the outcomes."

Assuming you put the **80/20** Rule right into your time usage plan, at that point you can concentrate for the day on your main concerns (the 20% that lead to 80% outcomes). You can then deal with different undertakings if and when you get an extra second.

Utilize "Technology's" Power in Strategy 3.

You ought to likewise use innovation to assist with staying on track and moving along as planned, as well as to achieve almost any undertaking you put your energy into.

The absolute best mechanical developments these days can be found in versatile applications. With a huge number of applications accessible in the Apple Application Store and Android Market, there are endless applications that can assist you with maintaining your business while in a hurry.

One illustration of an application that I like is called <u>Super Output</u>. This application makes it simple for me to convert papers and articles to PDF right from my iPhone. There is a compelling reason to stack records into a scanner with this application. You just point, snap, and catch the picture.

Also, that is only one straightforward illustration of the kinds of applications that are accessible today for cell phones. There are innumerable others, for example, streak light applications, banking applications, efficiency applications, exercise and nourishment applications, and millions more.

However, the central issue is that there really are astounding ways of involving innovation in your business. It's smart to occasionally return to your innovation needs to check whether some new piece of programming, equipment, or a versatile application can thoroughly change your business for an extremely plausible venture.

Combining the potential of leverage via all three of these tactics may significantly accelerate the growth of your company. Try them out for yourself to judge!

Mr. Thomas Boaz

CONCLUSION

The **secret weapon of wealth** is a combination of hard work, discipline, and smart decision-making. **Hard work** is essential to achieving success and building wealth. It requires dedication, focus, and a willingness to put in the effort to reach your goals. **Discipline** is also important in order to stay on track and make sure you are consistently working towards your goals.

Smart decision-making is also key to building wealth. This means understanding the risks and rewards of different investments, and making decisions that will help you reach your financial goals. Additionally, **having a plan** and **sticking to it** is essential to building wealth. This means setting goals, creating a budget, and tracking your progress. Finally, **having a positive attitude** and **staying motivated** is essential to achieving success and building wealth. With the right combination of **hard work**, **discipline**, and **smart decision-making**, you can be well on your way to building wealth and achieving financial success.

www.ingramcontent.com/pod-product-compliance
Lightning Source LLC
Chambersburg PA
CBHW071143220526
45467CB00015B/1811